Ace Guide to Holiday Packing

Andy Hind

Ace Guide to Holiday Packing

Olympia Publishers
London

www.olympiapublishers.com
OLYMPIA PAPERBACK EDITION

A CIP catalogue record for this title is
available from the British Library.

ISBN: 978-1-78830-945-5

First Published in 2022

Olympia Publishers
Tallis House
2 Tallis Street
London
EC4Y 0AB

Printed in Great Britain

Contents

Packing Lists
  Generic

Specific Types of Holidays

Foreword by Chris Packham CBE

'It's called organisation'. And when I deliver this cruel line to those who have 'forgotten' to pack some intrinsically essential item, like a phone charger, raincoat, or insect repellent, I do it looking down my nose with camp smugness and the most irritating wagging finger. Then I shake my head, tut, and walk away theatrically muttering about 'boots'. (The latter alludes to the famous scene in The Deer Hunter, where Stanley forgets his boots and Mike (Robert De Niro) refuses to lend him his spares.) When you've travelled halfway round the world and arrived up the creek, you just can't forget your paddle. You can't, It's not possible.

But people do. All the time. That's why pattern, process and practice need to be executed with ruthless efficiency. That's why lists are imperative – mental or literal. Before I go on, I'm going to come clean... I have twice forgotten things. Once, my travel hairdryer on a trip to arctic Canada, and secondly my binoculars – yes, yes, I know it's ridiculous, but it's true, I bloody well forgot my binoculars on a wildlife shoot! Hell, that hurt, still hurts. What an idiot.

To prevent such cataclysmic embarrassment I pack early, have pre-packed toiletries, (essentially a double set to avoid the need to raid the bathroom on the way out the door) and a bag with another double set of chargers, adaptor plugs etc. I lay it all out on the floor, mimicking an 'all you need to have to survive in x' photoshoot. Then I arrange it all meticulously in my cases, each item having a precise position, so that it's not only safe or accessible but also so that if it is absent that absence sticks out like a sore thumb.

Another absolute essential is 'double-bagging'. Rough baggage handlers and air pressure changes are apt to rupture cosmetic tubes with disastrous/hilarious results. I mean who would slip a half-used bottle of shampoo in between their best shirts at the last minute? The person who then opens their case to a find everything covered in a sticky soapy froth, that's who. Wrap your toiletries bag in a poly bag and wrap that in another. Double bagging... simple. In fact, an ample supply of zip lock bags is a must. That way, muddy socks, filthy shoes, chocolate – which melts you know – are all easily contained without contamination of all your other necessities.

My ultimate advice is simple. Follow Andy's advice. Make lists, tick boxes, plan, check, double check and whatever you do... double bag your shampoo!

Chris Packham

Introduction

Today we are taking more and more holidays. We all have our favourite and familiar places — especially for family holidays — and go back to them most years. But with easier access to an increasing number and variety of enticing destinations, one may be tempted to try fresh holiday places and ideas. However, having decided on where and what kind of holiday you're going to take, there always comes the nightmare of figuring out what you're going to need to take with you, with the attendant anxiety of forgetting to pack items vital to the enjoyment of your vacation. Never fear, it is more than likely that one or other of the lists I've compiled for this book will cover or assist you in the task of packing for your holiday.

All through my life, I've loved to travel. As a student and young man, most of my holidays were of the adventurous and sporting kind: cycling, canoeing, hiking and skiing. Pursuing these activities, I acquired the understanding and skill of packing the essentials, especially where weight and mobility were key elements. During my working life, I've been on all kinds of trips to all kinds of places, sometimes having to throw together an overnight bag in double-quick time, sometimes having to prepare for long stays to oversee projects in exotic (and often challenging) locations.

This book contains over 22 lists, based on my own experiences and those of friends and acquaintances who have helped me with their own suggestions. I have deliberately made it easy to use, because the simplest things always work the best.

She forgot to pack anything to read.

How to use this Book

The packing lists in this book may be more comprehensive than you need but you can add or delete as you wish because they are designed as aide-memoir rather than absolute requirements.

In first section the packing lists are Generic. These are intended for all holidays. They should be used in conjunction with the specific holiday lists found later in this book, whether your holiday is in the UK or abroad.

Each item has two checkboxes; one for 'To buy / find' and one 'Got it'. There are also extra lines and a blank sheet for you to add your own personal items. The author allows pages to be photocopied for the purpose of packing for your current holiday.

In every list there are USEFUL HINTS AND TIPS, indicated by a number in brackets, which explain or elaborate on the related item. The author has kept the footnotes as infrequent and basic as possible, as this book is not intended as a detailed travel guide.

Readers should be aware that this is, essentially, a book of lists of what to take, rather than what not to take with you when you go away. So – particularly when travelling abroad – it is strongly advised that you carefully consider any items or substances that might be regarded as illegal or problematic by the authorities there. For example, certain proprietary drugs that are perfectly legal in the UK (such as any that contain codeine) are banned in many other places. If you are in any doubt, it would be wise to check up on the embassy websites of the countries you intend to visit.

*To have traveled hopefully is a better thing
than to arrive.*

Before you Go

It seems that there is an endless number of chores that need to be ticked off before you travel, especially if your holiday or trip is going to take you abroad. From ordering medications in advance, to making sure you'll get to your departure point on time; from organizing insurance, to checking your passport's validity; all these details – and many more – need to be attended to. In fact, packing a case is almost the last thing you'll find yourself doing in preparation for going away.

This list is intended to help you make sure you don't miss anything crucial. It's designed to relieve your anxiety about the tiny details and help you avoid stress, so that you can actually look forward to your holiday rather than wishing you'd never booked to go away in the first place!

COUNTDOWN TO YOUR DEPARTURE	Done
1. Six months before going abroad 2. One month before 3. Two weeks before 4. Two days before 5. One day before 6. Medical 7. Up to date: insurance, travel documents and driving licences 8. Documents	
1. Six months before going abroad	
Make sure you have a passport with several blank pages that is valid for at least six months from the date of your departure. If not, send off for a replacement.	
Phone or visit your GP or health clinic to enquire about which vaccinations are required and how long in advance or check on a health website. Book an appointment for the vaccinations.	
Start investigating the language of the country you will be visiting or find a pocket-sized guide.	
If necessary, apply for visas.	

COUNTDOWN TO YOUR DEPARTURE	Done
2. One month before	
Visit a dentist. If you haven't had a check-up recently.	
Check the list in this book for the type of holiday you are going on for anything special you might need to buy.	
Check whether the airline will allow buggies for infants, sports equipment, e.g. skis to be placed in the hold. And whether they charge extra for this. If so, you might consider hiring at your destination. Check the airline's luggage restrictions. If taking on-board luggage only, check your case is the correct size.	
If you have pets, book kennels / cattery and check your pet's vaccination certificates are up to date.	
Take out travel insurance and check the policy will cover cancellation and also any sports, e.g., skiing, scuba diving, skydiving or activities you are planning to try on holiday.	
Check the Foreign Office's website for current travel advice: www.gov.uk/knowbeforeyougo	

COUNTDOWN TO YOUR DEPARTURE	Done
2. One month before	
If going to a malarial region, ask your GP or pharmacist for advice on which anti-malaria tablets to take. The NHS do not give tablets, but one can buy them over the counter without a prescription. They are very expensive, £34 for a pack of 24.	
Book car parking space or an overnight hotel and parking (can usually be a much better deal).	

The author allows this check page to be photocopied when packing for your current holiday

COUNTDOWN TO YOUR DEPARTURE	Done
3. Two weeks before	
If you are going into a malarial region, check when you need to start taking the anti-malaria medication.	
Check whether your pets need to visit a vet.	
Buy the local currency of your destination before you travel.	
Book your seats on the plane. Print out two sets of e-tickets and boarding passes if required. Place them in different bags. Some airlines do not allow you to do this more than the day before.	
Give your itinerary to a friend or neighbour with landline contact numbers if possible.	
Inform your credit card companies when and where you are going and get a reference reply confirming that you have told them.	
On your return, if you have used them, check your credit / debit card bills for unexpected charges (particularly from car hire companies). You have ten days to complain about the charges and if the card company can't justify the charges, then the card company should reimburse them to you. Try to use local currency wherever possible, especially in restaurants if the bill is relatively small.	

COUNTDOWN TO YOUR DEPARTURE	Done
4. Two days before	
Start to pack.	
Confirm your flight.	
Confirm check-in time.	
Book taxi and / or check train times, especially on a weekend or public holidays.	
Check for news of strikes / road hold-ups / train delays / planned engineering works.	

The author allows this check page to be photocopied when packing for your current holiday

COUNTDOWN TO YOUR DEPARTURE	Done
5. One day before	
Before finally loading your case, lay out your outfits - all of them, including suitable shoes and accessories for said outfit - even if you chose to wear them on a different day it means you know you have something for every day and for the 'events' you might be attending.	
Go over the checklist one last time.	
Finish packing.	

COUNTDOWN TO YOUR DEPARTURE	Done
6. Medical	
At least six months before you travel check with your GP's surgery which vaccinations you require and what health precautions you need to take. It is important to obtain advice about any possible reactions you might have to vaccinations, which could delay your departure. Make sure that your immunization booklet and / or vaccination certificates are up to date. Ask about remedies for travel sickness if you suffer from this condition.	
If you need to carry syringes (e.g., for diabetes), obtain a letter confirming that you need these from your GP. Inform the airline that you have injections with you when you check in, rather than when you go through security, so that they have time to check your documents.	
Ask your GP whether the medication that you are taking is affected by extreme temperatures, altitude, or any other unusual environmental factors (e.g., humidity).	
If going to a malarial region, ask your GP's or pharmacist advice on which anti-malaria tablets to take. The NHS do not give tablets, but one can buy them without a prescription. You may need to start taking them before you go.	
If you are going on a long-haul fight, ask your GP about the risk of deep vein thrombosis (DVT), and check whether you need to take aspirin or wear compression stockings.	

COUNTDOWN TO YOUR DEPARTURE	Done
6. Medical	
Phone either the embassy of your destination or the UK Home Office (tel. 020 7035 0472 / 0476) to check that your medication can be legally taken into that country or whether there are any restrictions on its use. For example, the drug codeine (which is also known as methyl morphine, as well as having several brand names) must be in the form of tablets containing less than 100 mg. In some countries codeine is banned, and there have been cases of people having been arrested and jailed for having codeine tablets on them, and in one case (in the United Arab Emirates) for having traces of the drug in their urine.	

COUNTDOWN TO YOUR DEPARTURE	Done
7. Up-to-date: insurance, travel documents and driving licences	
Make sure you have up-to-date comprehensive travel and medical insurance, which is valid for the countries and activities you have planned. Check that the insurance covers you if you are pregnant.	
Some activities, such as bungee jumping, hot air ballooning, quad biking, riding on a scooter or motorbike (over 50cc), may have to be specifically mentioned by you.	
If you are going to an island which has volcanic activity, e.g., Madeira, then you will need a Helicopter Evacuation Insurance.	
Be sure your policy provides for:	
An air ambulance, in case you need to be flown home.	
All medical bills (which can be expensive).	
Any pre-existing medical conditions	
Any potentially hazardous sports activities.	
Bringing the body home, in the event of a death.	
Bringing your family home, in the event of your illness or injury.	
Replacing and / or bringing your car home.	

COUNTDOWN TO YOUR DEPARTURE	Done
8. Documents	
Passport with at least six months' validity. Make sure that the next-of-kin section is filled in and is up to date.	
Another means of photo identification, e.g., UK Driving Licence, expired passport (this could be essential to get a replacement passport if you lose or have your passport stolen as proof of citizenship).	
Visa: Contact the relevant embassies and apply at least six months in advance.	
International Driving Licence: Check with a motoring organisation if this is necessary for the country you will be driving in.	
International Student Identity Card / YHA Card.	
Photocopies of everything important (passports, travellers' cheque numbers, etc.). Leave a copy at home, on the Internet (email or cloud) and, if possible, with your travelling companion. You could copy all the information on to a memory stick or phone memory as another back-up of your essential information, BUT remember, if someone steals this then they have access to it and could use it against you. It is much safer on the Internet. Could also have a Dropbox account, One Drive or Google Drive storage.	

COUNTDOWN TO YOUR DEPARTURE	Done
Suggestions for copies of documents to store on the Internet on your email account (emails sent to yourself with document attached).	
Emergency phone numbers, email and postal addresses.	
Travel insurance: Some companies can offer a booklet in PDF format that explains their policies.	
Driving Licence - International. Take the plastic card – the paper section is no longer issued, but is available to view online.	
Car insurance, this is now available online.	
Car registration documents and / or proof of ownership, this is now available online.	
Car breakdown insurance.	
Green card insurance form.	
Credit / debit card insurance.	
Passport for each traveller / family member.	
Your personal address database.	
Recent utility bill for proof of address.	
Medical details for each member of the family – GP details, blood group, generic names of drugs being taken, glasses prescriptions, and copy of vaccination certificates.	

The author allows this check page to be photocopied when packing for your current holiday

COUNTDOWN TO YOUR DEPARTURE	Done
Receipts of expensive items, such as cameras and laptops, as proof of having bought them in the UK.	
Make sure that the password you use for your email or cloud site is unique and not the one you use for everything else.	
Make sure that someone else knows your password, in case you become unconscious, and access is required to your email account or documents.	

The Essentials

This is an essential packing list for all holidays and should be used in conjunction with the specific holiday lists, whether in the UK or abroad.

Be aware, however, that if you take everything on this list, you will go way over the suitcase luggage allowance and may have a lot of things you don't need: for example, most hotels have a hairdryer in their bathrooms or can supply one on demand, so it is important to select only those items you really need.

Some of the items listed here could go into the Flight Bag List 07 and medication items into the Medical List 09.

Remember the mantra: Pack 'must have it' items, not 'just in case' stuff.

	To find / buy	Got it
This list is in eight parts to help you find items: 1. Documents, paper items 2. General clothes for both men and women 3. General items 4. Products 5. Toiletry items 6. Travelling by car 7. Money 8. Miscellaneous		
1. Documents, paper items		
Address book[1]		
Diary		
Driving Licence – International[2]		
Guidebook, one with local laws in it[3]		
Hotel reservations confirmation		
Insurance: car breakdown card		
Insurance: car insurance certificate – this will be online		
Insurance: travel insurance documents		
Itinerary[4]		
MOT certificate – this will be online		
Notebook and pen		
Passport(s), check if current [5]		
Phrase book, if going abroad		
Reading material		

	To find / buy	Got it
2. General clothes for men and women[6]		
Belts		
Boots / wellingtons (if travelling by car)		
Casual and smart outfits for daytime / evening		
Ear warmers / muffs for winter breaks		
Fleece or heavy woollens for winter breaks		
Formal dress for evening dinners		
Gloves (optional)		
Hat, caps (optional)		
Laundry bag[7]		
Laundry soap		
Raincoat / jacket / anorak		
Scarf (optional)		
Sewing kit, needle and thread, mending kit, safety pins		
Shirts and ties or blouses and cardigans		
Shoe polish kit		
Shoes and socks / heeled shoes and tights / trainers		
Sleeping kit: pyjama / nightdress, shorts, bed socks		

06 - The Essentials

	To find / buy	Got it
Sunhat, e.g., baseball cap		
Swimsuits / cover-up tops		
Travel outfit (loose fitting, light)[8]		
Trousers, jeans and leggings		
Underwear		

	To find / buy	Got it
3. General items		
Alarm clock[9] (or mobile phone) – Radio controlled clocks[10]		
Batteries, spare, for camera / camcorder		
Binoculars, small pair		
Body camera, GoPro®		
Bum bags[14]		
Camera / camcorder[11]		
Camera, disposable underwater		
Chargers[12]		
Electrical socket travel adaptors[13]		
Kindle / tablet		
Laptop		
Luggage scales		
Memory stick		
Sunglasses and case, prescription if needed		

	To find / buy	Got it
4. Products		
Contact lenses: spare pair or daily disposable and contact lens lubricant. If you are going to somewhere dusty then take more than you normally would, or take glasses.		
Glasses and a spare pair		
Medication, see Medical List 09 Stain removal fluid / wipes		
Sun protection cream or spray		
Sunburn treatment cream, Aloe Vera gel, Nivea® moisturising cream		
Wet wipes and / or hand-cleaning fluid		

	To find / buy	Got it
5. Toiletries		
Bathroom wash bag(s), see Toiletries and Wash Bag List 08		
Beauty care items – see Toiletries and Wash Bag List 08		
Ear plugs		
Flannel / sponge		
Hairdryer (optional)		
Hair ties and grips		
Sleep eye mask		

	To find / buy	Got it
6. Travelling by car		
If travelling by car in some countries (e.g., France), by law you must carry some of the following items: • Breakdown triangle • Breath analyser (requirement in France) • Green card for continental driving • High visibility jacket for driver, accessible from inside the car • High visibility jackets for each passenger, if required • Relevant maps • Space blanket • Spare bulbs • Valid breakdown cover NB For the most recent advice, it is best to check a motoring organisation website for the country you are going to be driving through.		

	To find / buy	Got it
7. Money		
Credit cards		
Currency[15]		
Decoy wallet with some small notes / change in it		
Mobile phone and charger		
Money belt, possibly a waterproof one for swimming or water sports		
Money, small change[16]		

	To find / buy	Got it
8. Miscellaneous		
Accommodation [23]		
Beach towel / bath sheet		
Door stop and sink plug[17]		
Gaffer tape / duct tape, small roll, black and white		
Keys for suitcase(s)		
Keys, spare set for house and car, or leave with neighbour		
Knife, multi-purpose (e.g., Gerber®, Victorinox®, Leatherman®)[18]		
Luggage identity labels for suitcases and flight bag[19]		
Padlock – combination type		
Plug, universal bath / sink		
Shoulder bag or small backpack		
Smoke and carbon monoxide detector[20]		
Torch, e.g., pencil Maglite® or a wind-up one if you have one		
Suitcases[19]		
Travel iron		
Travel speakers		
Umbrella		
Wedding ring[21]		
Whistle to frighten off stray dogs or alone in the dark and need to attract attention		
Wire coat hangers[22]		

	To find / buy	Got it
Wristwatch, cheap one		

#	USEFUL HINTS AND TIPS
1	**Address book**
	For postcards and emergency contact information. Alternatively, ensure these details are on your mobile and backed up on a memory stick.
	Also make a note of the details for the British Embassy, High Commission or Consulate for the countries you are going to or travelling through before you leave.
2	**Driving Licence – International**
	Check www.dh.gov.uk for a full list of countries.
3	**Guidebooks**
	Find one with local laws and customs in it – check local dos and don'ts.
4	**Itinerary**
	Some non-EU countries will not let you in without a guarantee of when you intend to leave.
5	**Passports**
	Some countries require that visitors' passports have at least six months on them before they expire.
	You could take an old passport for identification purposes and leave the current one in the hotel safe. An expired passport would be essential to get a replacement passport if you lose or have it stolen as proof of citizenship.

6   Clothes

The amount of clothes you should take is not included, as this depends on personal preference. It would be useful to make notes about what you use while on holiday and adjust your list accordingly.

Remember that you can use local laundries. Most modern hotels offer same-day services and in cities local laundry establishments will offer good value.

7   Laundry bag

You could take two or three small plastic bags; also put one or two in your flight bag, just in case your suitcase bursts open.

8   Travel clothes

Put to one side the set of clothes you intend to travel in – light, loose clothing is best when flying. Have several layers so you can peel them off as required. Combat trousers are good as they are usually loose-fitting and have pockets on the leg which are easy to reach when you are strapped into your seat. Do not have camouflaged as in some countries these are only for the military.

9   Alarm clock

Your mobile phone is ideal for this, but make sure it is fully charged.

I have had a Westclox® Travelmate folding alarm clock for years, batteries last for a year at least.

10   Radio-controlled clocks.

In most cases pre-tuned radio-controlled clocks sold in the UK are pre-tuned to the UK transmitter, however, it depends on what type of receiver the clock has if it will correct to the country you are in.

It may stay on UK time or revert to UK time, even if you manually change to the local time. So the best advice is not to take a radio-controlled clock unless you are sure it will keep to local time.

If you factory reset, the clock will remain on the time you set it at.

11   Memory cards

Take extra camera memory cards – buy the largest one you can afford.

If your weight allowance will allow, you could take a tablet / laptop and download your photos onto that. Then sort them, label them and file them while abroad to clear your camera's memory and while you have the enthusiasm to do so.

12   Chargers

Charge up before you go and take all necessary chargers.

13   Electrical socket

Electrical socket travel adaptors (these can be purchased at the airport). Some now have an integral USB socket for charging a phone.

14   Money Belts

If taking large amounts of cash, it is best to wear money belts underneath external clothing.

15   **Currency**

Buy the currency of the country you are visiting before you go. Sometimes it's useful to take a small amount of a strong currency.

One way to use up your local currency when leaving your holiday resort abroad is to pay the hotel room bill with all the local currency you have left. If there is still something to pay, use a credit card, but remember you may need some at the airport or for transport to the airport.

16   **Money / small change**

Make sure you have some loose change for the airport trolley, ticket machines, taxi fares, tips etc.

17   **Doorstop**

To add security to a hotel door or a B&B where there is no lock, a rubber doorstop / wedge could be used to prevent it being opened from the outside.

18   **Knife / Scissors**

Multi-purpose Swiss Army knife (e.g., Gerber®, Victorinox®, Leatherman®).

Do not attempt to take any knives / scissors in your hand luggage onto a plane, even a tiny keyring knife or it will be confiscated at the airport security desk.

19   **Suitcases**

Airline luggage over 23kg is considered to be heavy luggage – the absolute maximum a suitcase can weigh is 32kg. If your suitcase is over this limit then it could be considered freight and might have to be sent as unaccompanied luggage.

Use a lockable case with wheels. If going to the USA, be sure to buy one that the TSA (Transportation Security Administration) can open.

If you intend to bring back goods, then pack a small case/bag and put it inside a larger case when travelling out.

Suitcase straps: in a bright colour or hi vis, so it's easy to recognise your case at the airport baggage reclaim.

Luggage label / tag / business card holder. For security, make sure that it is one that cannot be read unless you lift a flap covering your name and address.

20   **Smoke alarm**

Some small B & Bs may not have the fire alarm systems which guesthouses and hotels have. They may not even have any smoke alarms in the house, so it's a good idea to take a small domestic one if you are nervous of fire breaking out.

An added precaution if renting abroad is to take a combination smoke and carbon monoxide detector.

21   **Wedding ring**

For women, especially those travelling alone, if you are not married then consider wearing a wedding ring as it can help you avoid harassment.

22	**Wire coat hangers**

Take at least six and leave them behind! Not all hotels have enough hangers in their wardrobes, although you could ask reception for more.

23	**Accommodation / hotel facilities**

For e.g. is there a hot tub, do I need to pack swimwear? Do I want to use the gym facilities? Do I need to pack my own towel, or would the hotel provide one?

Addendum

Hotel address tip

When you arrive at a hotel in an unfamiliar city or town and if you do not speak the language, then take one of the hotel cards, write your name on it (not room number) and put it into your wallet or purse. If you get lost, you can show it to a taxi driver; if you are taken ill, the authorities can find out who you are and where you are staying.

In-Flight Bag
for short and long-haul flights

Even the most frequent of flyers has experienced the aggravation of suddenly realising that something you need during the flight is packed away in your suitcase and stowed – secure but unreachable – in the aircraft's hold.

So here's a list of things you might want to keep with you, not just during your flight but also while you wait in the departure lounge.

Before you go, check the airline's flight bag size. It is usually only one bag / cabin case per person. Most airlines have the same size bag dimensions as this is dictated by the plane.

For most airlines, you are also allowed another bag which will fit easily underneath your seat.

And remember, NO dangerous items of sharp objects such as key ring pen knives, nail scissors etc. are allowed in your in-flight bags.[1]

	To find / buy	Got it
Camera		
Contact lenses (if used)		
Credit / debit cards		
Driving Licence – International		
Ear plugs		
Eye mask		
Eyeglasses		
Eyeglasses: spare pair and case		
Handbag with hairbrush or comb, make-up bag and other personal items		
House keys		
iPod / tablet / laptop		
Jumper, woolly or fleece, shawl (it can get cold on a plane)		
Laundry bag[2]		
Lip balm		
Luggage identity labels on bags		
Make-up items in bag		
Medication in blister packs,[3] see Medical List 09		
Memory stick		
Mobile phone		
Purse / wallet / cash carrier / small change for drinks		
Notebook and pen (optional)		
Paper tissues		

	To find / buy	Got it
Passport		
Playing cards[4]		
Reading material		
Spare underwear and toothbrush (in case your luggage is mislaid on arrival)		
Sunglasses		
Toiletry bottles[5]		
Travel alarm		
Travel insurance documents		
Travel tickets / boarding cards. Print out e-tickets and boarding passes if required.		
Umbrella, small (optional)		
Water bottle: Buy after you have gone through security checks.		
Wet wipes or foam hand wash		

	To find / buy	Got it
Long-haul flights		
Eye mask[6]		
Flight socks for long haul – these are tight to improve the circulation and to prevent DVT (deep vein thrombosis).		
Good pair of ear plugs		
Neck pillow		
Slippers or warm socks (some airlines provide these on long flights)		
Toilette bag with toothbrush, freshen-up wipes, lip balm, etc.		
Wool jumper		

#	USEFUL HINTS AND TIPS

1   Hand Luggage

Other items which cannot be taken on board as hand luggage. If in doubt, check before you go on the airline's website.

Here are some other items which **CANNOT** be taken on board as hand luggage. If in doubt, check before you go on the airline's website.

- Bat, racket, or sports stick
- Catapult
- Crash helmet, could also include skiing and cycling helmets
- Darts
- Fishing rod
- Golf clubs
- Knitting needles
- Picture frames with glass
- Snooker, pool or billiard cue
- Walking / hiking poles

2   Laundry bag

Take 1 or 2 laundry or dust bin bags, just in case your suitcase bursts open, or you are over your weight allowance and need to take some items out.

3   Medication in blister packs

Pack all your medications in your in-flight bag.

Make sure you have enough medication in your in-flight bag so if your main luggage goes astray you will have sufficient to last until you are able to buy some more.

Travel sickness remedies: see Medical List 09 for more information.

4   **Playing cards**

Playing cards, crossword puzzles, Sudoku, dice or some other portable entertainment, as a change to reading material, in case you have to wait in the departure lounge for delayed flights or transfers.

5   **Toiletry bottles**

There are restrictions on the volume of liquids you can take in your hand luggage so check the airline's website.

Here are some issues you might need to consider:

Containers must hold no more than 100 ml.

Containers must be in a single, transparent, re-sealable plastic bag, which holds no more than a litre and measures approximately 20cm x 20cm.

Contents must fit comfortably inside the bag so it can be sealed.

Bags must not be knotted or tied at the top.

You are limited to 1 plastic bag per person.

You must show the bag to airport security when going through security control.

Have a transparent bathroom bag to keep all these in.

6   Eye mask

For long waits in departure lounges

To help me rest I have found a stretchy headband (for example, the ones which are in a decorative material, used on skiing holidays) very good for keeping out light and noise as you can pull it up and leave it there and you don't look too stupid. Or a woolly hat can be pulled down over your eyes and also your ears.

However, do be aware of theft if you are going to sleep, and make sure your valuables are on you.

Toiletries & Washbag

It's only when we plan to go away that most of us suddenly realise just how many toiletry items we've actually got in the bathroom. And there's one factor they often all have in common: they're heavy! Of course, you'll want to look your best and be at your freshest, and that means you'll have personal choices in deodorants and / or make-up that you'll want to take with you.

However, it's worth remembering there'll probably be perfectly well-stocked pharmacies in most destinations. And – particularly if you're going on a short trip – you'll find a lot of chemists and stores now offer special travel-size tubes, bottles and cans of the most commonly-used toiletries.

So the less you take with you, the lighter your suitcase and the easier travelling will be.

	To find / buy	Got it
After sun cream / lotion, e.g., Aloe Vera		
Anti-perspirant / deodorant		
Antiseptic liquid		
Body lotion (optional)		
Contact lenses (and a spare pair), contact lens fluid		
Cotton buds and cotton wool pads (for make-up removal)		
Dental floss / picks		
Earplugs		
Eye shade		
Face scrub exfoliator (optional)		
Family planning requirements		
Flannel / wash cloth / wet wipes		
Hairbrush (only if not in handbag / flight bag)		
Hand cream (only if not in-flight bag)		
Hand sanitiser / cleanser		
Hand soap in container		
Lip care		
Make-up removal cream / lotion		
Manicure kit		
Medication – see Medical List 09		
Mirror, hand – unbreakable		
Mouthwash		
Nail brush		

	To find / buy	Got it
Nail clippers		
Plasters		
Razor, and a spare		
Roll of medical tape		
Scissors – small pair with blunt ends		
Shampoo and conditioner in small containers		
Shower cap		
Shower gel		
Sunscreen cream / lotion, small size		
Talcum powder (optional)		
Tissues, small packet (could be put in case)		
Toothbrush		
Toothpaste		
Travel sewing kit		
Tube of lubricating jelly		
Tweezers		

	To find / buy	Got it
For men		
Aftershave		
Electric shaver and charger / lead		
Pre-electric shaver lotion		
Shaving brush		
Shaving gel		
Styptic pencil (for shaving cuts)		

	To find / buy	Got it
For women		
Hair straighteners and / or heated rollers		
Make-up bag (in flight bag or handbag now)		
Make-up removal cream / lotion		
Menstrual supplies		
Moisturisers and toners (Facial care creams)		
Nail file (could be in handbag / flight bag)		
Nail polish and remover		
Perfume		

Medical Items

Plenty of specialist travel books and websites cover this subject exhaustively but I have found there are a number of critical dos and don'ts when it comes to health issues. For example, many family holidays are marred from the day of arrival in hotter climes, when excited youngsters rush off into the great outdoors without adequate protection from the sun's rays. So pack suitable sun protection cream or spray for children. You will need an SPF of at least 30 and preferably 50 with a UVA rating of 4 – 5 to prevent youngsters becoming lobsters and having a painful time. The long-term risks of sunburn must also be considered. Check that your sunscreen is still in date and effective. Stay hydrated...

PRESCRIPTIONS:
If you need medication on a regular basis, add any drugs / treatments in the space at the end of this list: and be sure to order enough, in advance, to see you through your stay. It's wise to speak to your GP and / or pharmacist before you travel (especially to tropical destinations) to check if your medication might be affected by extreme temperatures. And for certain destinations ask your GP for a signed letter (with a phone number on it) certifying which drugs you're using and why. It is worth taking a copy of your prescriptions, too. Customs officials may require validation of any controlled drugs; besides, you could find you need more while you're away.

MEDICAL EXPENSES:

Check whether your insurance cover will enable you to recoup any large outlays or emergency hospitalization.

If you are travelling to a developing country, you might consider taking a medical pack containing sterile syringes and other essential items for any serious accident, as these can be in short supply.

The NHS do not give medication for malaria. These must be brought yourself. If going to a malarial region, ask your GP or pharmacist for advice on which anti-malaria tablets to take.

The NHS do not give medication for malaria, but one can buy tablets over the counter without a prescription. They are very expensive, £34 for a pack of 24.

	To find / buy	Got it
Acu-Strap™ travel wristbands[1]		
Altitude-sickness tablets (if intending to be at altitude)		
Antifungal cream or powder		
Antihistamines		
Anti-malaria tablets[2]		
Anti-nausea drugs		
Antiseptic wipes or cream		
Any medication / drugs that you regularly take or might need to take		
Arnica (to treat swelling, bruising, and / or inflammation)		
Aspirin for DVT (Deep Vein Thrombosis) (check with your GP first)		
Asthma medication		
Blister patches (e.g., Compeed®)		
Calamine lotion		
Ciprofloxacin[3]		
Contact lenses, solutions, and saline		
Freeze spray (or cream) to relieve muscular discomfort		
Ginger biscuits and / or ginger beer (to relieve travel sickness and motion sickness)		
Heartburn and indigestion remedies		
Cream to relieve insect bites, Hydrocortisone cream for mosquito bites		

	To find / buy	Got it
Ibuprofen tablets (to treat swelling, bruising, and / or inflammation)		
Ice bag (to reduce inflammation caused by injuries)		
Insect repellent sprays / creams		
Iodine tablets (for sterilizing water)		
Laxatives / loperamide		
Medicated pain relief plasters		
Mosquito coils (if appropriate to your destination)		
Moisturising cream (Nivea®)		
Pain relief e.g., Paracetamol (for reducing temperature) and / or Ibuprofen		
Plastic syringe and spoon		
Rehydration sachets		
Sunburn treatment: Aloe Vera gel and for pain relief Solarcaine®		
Travel-sickness: motion-sickness tablets[4]		
Vaccination card or record, and medical certificates		

#	USEFUL HINTS AND TIPS

1 **Acu-Strap™ travel wristbands**

Acu-Strap™ travel wristbands and children's identity bracelets that list the child's medical requirements.

Ideally these should be written in the language of the country you are visiting and include contact phone numbers and the full address of the place where you are staying.

2 **Anti-malaria tablets**

Anti-malaria tablets. If going to a malarial region, ask your GPs or pharmacist for advice on which anti-malaria tablets to take. The NHS do not give tablets, but you can buy them over the counter without a prescription.

3 **Ciprofloxacin**

Ciprofloxacin (to treat traveller's diarrhoea, 'Delhi belly'); discuss its use with your GP before you travel.

4 **Travel-sickness: motion-sickness tablets**

Ginger biscuits and / or ginger beer (to relieve travel sickness and motion sickness). May need to wear a Motion Sickness Band.

Useful telephone numbers and websites

Home Office
www.homeoffice.gov.uk

Drugs Branch: + 44 (0) 20 7035 0472 / 76 to find out which medicines you can take in or out of the UK and your destination country.

National Health Service (NHS)

Apply for a UK Global Health Insurance Card (UK GHIC) www.gov.uk/travel-abroad

Health advice and information is available 24 hours a day from NHS 111 by calling 111.

First Aid Kits

Anyone who thinks it's desirable or possible to guard against every injury or sickness while on holiday should invest here and now in a fully equipped ambulance and paramedic team to accompany them on their travels. Truth to tell, it's only worth trying to anticipate those accidents and emergencies that are most likely to happen. So consider the kind of climates, regions and activities you're about to encounter on your trip or holiday. You probably will not have to deal with jellyfish stings if you're going skiing, for instance, or take high altitude sickness tablets with you when going scuba diving.

If you already have a First Aid box that you usually take with you on holiday, don't just pop it in the case and assume you're covered – check to see if you need to replenish any of the contents.

Some of these items will also be found on previous packing lists.

	To find / buy	Got it
General First Aid Kit contents		
Antihistamine tablets		
Antiseptic cream		
Antiseptic wipes		
Bite and sting cream		
Blister dressing		
Burn cream		
Cold and flu tablets		
Corn pads		
Cotton buds		
Cotton wool		
Crepe bandage		
Diarrhoea tablets[1]		
Dioralyle® rehydration sachets		
Elasticated support bandage		
Elastic wrap bandage		
Indigestion tablets		
Iodine or TCP (for small cuts etc.)		
Malaria pills		
Melolin dressings (non-sticky)		
Micropore tape		
Motion sickness tablets		
One large wound dressing pack		
One pair of disposable latex gloves		
Pack of wound closure strips		

0 - First Aid

	To find / buy	Got it
Pain medication e.g., Paracetamol, Ibuprofen		
Plasters, bandages and dressings		
Rehydration tablets or sachets		
Safety pins		
Scissors, small pair		
Space blanket (for mountain climbing / skiing / emergencies)		
Thermometer, strip or disposable		
Tubular bandages		
Tweezers		
Vaseline (for ticks / cracked heels)		
Vinegar (sachets)[2]		

	To find / buy	Got it

The author allows this check page to be photocopied when packing for your current holiday

#	USEFUL HINTS AND TIPS
1	**Diarrhoea tablets** Ciprofloxacin (to treat traveller's diarrhoea, 'Delhi belly'); discuss its use with your GP before you travel.
2	**Vinegar** Vinegar: for jellyfish stings. Vinegar can be carried in small sachets like the ones you find in motorway service stations.

Parents and Children

Introduction

If you're travelling with children, decisions about what (or what not) to take with you become more complicated. Many of these choices will depend on the age of the children you're travelling with, which is why this section is divided into three parts.

Indeed, it could be subdivided almost ad infinitum, given that children's needs change so fast. So it's necessary to consider both their bodily needs and their boredom thresholds. The three parts of this section are:

- General List
- Infants and Pre-School Children
- School-age Children

Of course, no-one can know your children better than you. But these lists contain the collected wisdom and experience of many different mums and dads. And the piece of advice that crops up most consistently is that an unhappy child on holiday will almost certainly result in unhappy parents!

Parents and Children

General

The following list is a rough guide intended to cover the basic requirements for travelling or holidaying with children. The journey alone can be a real challenge, especially with younger children who have little concept of time. Children may also need plenty of distracting and / or comforting in the unfamiliar surroundings of, say, the cabin of an airliner.

It's worth stressing the need to take effective sun protection, a child's skin is far more delicate and sensitive than that of an adult, and the younger the child, the more susceptible they will be to sunburn and sunstroke.

Please note that most airlines won't carry a woman who is more than 36 weeks pregnant. A medical certificate may be required from the 28th week.

Expectant mothers should bring a copy of their hospital notes in case of emergency.

	To find / buy	Got it
Adoption papers (if applicable)		
After sun cream / lotion, e.g., Aloe Vera		
Anti-perspirant / deodorant		
Antiseptic liquid		
Body lotion (optional)		
Bedding (check that a cot etc. will be provided, and usually bedding is too)		
CDs or similar media with nursery rhymes, stories, videos or game players, hand-held, for their individual amusement on long car journeys.		
Comfortable and bright clothes for travelling out in [1]		
Consent letter (if both parents not present) [2]		
Cuddly toy – favourite toy or item such as a blanket! [3]		
Hats, UV protected		
Hooded towel		
Identity bracelet [4]		
Kid's sun block (lotion or spray), minimum sun protection factor SPF 25		
Medical items, see list 09		
Passports for each child		
Plastic (jelly) shoes for beach / swimming		
Play tent, UV protected		
Something to suck or chew for take-off and landing if flying		

2 - Parents and Children - General

	To find / buy	Got it
Sunglasses – must have a minimum UV 400 rating		
Swimming costume, possibly with in-built buoyancy aids		
Swimming goggles		
Swimwear, high-necked, UV protected		
Water buoyancy aids		

12 - Parents and Children - General

	To find / buy	Got it

#	USEFUL HINTS AND TIPS

1   **Travel clothes**

Dress young children in comfortable and brightly coloured clothing so you can easily spot them if they wander away from you. You could give them a brightly coloured top or baseball cap.

2   **Consent letter**

Currently, if you are travelling as a single parent, some countries will ask for proof that you have the consent of the other parent for the child to enter or leave their country.

Passports are now required for everyone in all countries: babies and children can no longer travel on their parent's passport.

You could also take the child's birth certificate.

3   **Cuddly toy**

As well as their favourite cuddly toy or blanket, you could take a spare toy or item in case this is lost.

A friend of mine had a boy who took a blanket everywhere he went. Knowing how upset her son would be if he lost it, she cut the blanket into two pieces. Her son never noticed, and she had a spare one.

4   **Identity bracelet**

If necessary, an identity bracelet – with the child's medical requirements. If possible, it should be in the language of the country you are visiting. Include contact numbers and your hotel's address.

Parents with Infants
and Pre-School Children

If you have a baby or a toddler, you'll probably have a well-worked out routine for looking after her or him already. And you'll no doubt already be aware that transporting and tending to them anywhere other than home entails forethought and – quite often – a logistical exercise of military proportions. So you'll have a pretty good idea of the basic items you need to take away if you're going on holiday.

However, because you'll have your hands full looking after your child right up to the time you depart for your holiday, it's easy enough to overlook vital pieces of paraphernalia – anything from a favoured potty to the old tea towel that your son has chosen to be his security blanket.

My advice is to check, check and check again!

	To find / buy	Got it
Packing list for un-weaned babies:		
Baby monitor – audio		
Baby sling for carrying on the beach, around town etc.		
Baby toiletries		
Bags, re-sealable plastic bags		
Barrier cream for nappy rash		
Breast pads, expressing machine and nipple cream, if breast-feeding		
Buggy (and shade / umbrella)		
Car seat (if flying and hiring a car – you may need to check whether seats should be forward or rear-facing)		
Car – rear view mirror for passenger to see children in the back		
Child carrier – backpack style		
Cot – hand-held carry cot, could double up as a bed		
First aid kit – see First Aid list 10 for parents with babies		
Formula and bottles, if bottle feeding		
Formula, ready-made, for flight and emergencies		
Nappies / wipes – take your favourite brand if necessary as they might not have them where you are going		
Plastic bedding sheet		

	To find / buy	Got it
Plastic changing sheet		
Potty liners		
Potty, portable		
Pram / crib mosquito net		
Soothers / comforters		
Sterilising equipment (if baby under 12 months), such as tablets or microwaveable steriliser bags		
Swim nappies and swimsuits		

	To find / buy	Got it
Changing Bag List:		
Changing mat – portable		
Cotton wool for new-borns		
Gauze squares, linen type		
Nappies, day and night, fewer if not for new-born		
Nappy barrier cream		
Nappy nippas or pins, if nappies don't have their own fastenings		
Nappy sacks		
Paper liners or, for ease of changing, fleece liners		
Tea tree oil [4]		
Wipes		

	To find / buy	Got it
Packing list for weaned babies **As previous page, plus:**		
Baby rice, rice cakes, and other snacks		
Bibs		
Jars of baby food (if unsure of availability abroad), check if allowed on plane.		
Plates, bowls, sippy cups etc.		
Portable booster seat / highchair [1]		
Soft spoons and cutlery		
Holiday Toddler Bag		
Kids out of nappies may need several pairs of trainer pants for the journey		
Travel entertainment		
Buggy [2]		
Car seat (if flying and hiring a car – you may need to check whether seats should be forward or rear-facing)		
Ear plugs specially designed for children		
Favourite toys, books, stickers and travel games		
Headphones		

13 - Parents with Infants and Pre-School Children

	To find / buy	Got it
In a car		
Magnetic board games		
Handheld games console or tablet		
iPad		
On a plane		
Own food [3]		

#	USEFUL HINTS AND TIPS

1 Portable booster seat / highchair

Portable booster seat / highchair, or a chair that wraps around or can clip onto the edge of most tables. This saves having to sit a child on your lap to feed them.

2 Buggies

Check with the airline BEFORE you go, to see what they will allow you to take on board and what will happen coming back.

On some airlines, buggies may be taken right up to the plane door and are then loaded into the hold. Most modern airlines do not include buggies and travel cots in your luggage allowance. If your baby / child has their own seat, they are allowed their own luggage allowance. You are also allowed one piece of hand luggage per passenger.

3 Own food

Airlines may provide a children's meal, but it may not be to their liking so it's best to pack a suitable snack such as bananas, and drinks, which they will like.

4 Tea tree oil

Tea tree, also known as melaleuca, is well-known for its powerful antiseptic properties and ability to treat wounds.

Aloe Vera Gel with Tea Tree Oil cleanses, softens and helps restore dry and damaged skin. It can be used for treatment of dry, chapped skin, sun burn, skin irritations and minor burns.

Parents and
School-Aged Children

Depending on whether you are driving, flying or going by train, your luggage allowances will differ tremendously. Once again, age is a key factor when deciding what a school-age child can bring (or be allowed to bring) with them. And of course, gender begins to be important. The needs of an eight-year-old boy will be very different to those of a fourteen-year-old girl. Obviously, weight and space mean you can't afford to let them bring everything they want, but if you explain this and ask them to think hard about what they feel they really can't do without for a week or two, it will help concentrate their minds.

It may be that one of the things they most want to bring with them is a best friend. This could be a good idea but it does place more responsibility directly on your shoulders. Make sure you check and bring things like insurance cover, letters of permission from their parents and identity documents. You won't want your holiday interrupted by lengthy and tedious discussions with border officials or local police.

	To find / buy	Got it
Bats and balls		
Bikes (if travelling by car)		
Boots, if walking is likely		
Car – rear view mirror for passenger (to see children in the back)		
Car seat in hire car [1]		
Eating utensils [2]		
Electronic audio equipment [3]		
First aid kit – see List 10		
Fishing nets		
Flasks		
Football		
Hats, UV protected		
Picnic equipment		
Play tent, UV protected		
Portable booster seat [4]		
Raincoats and hats		
Rucksack, a small one for each child [5]		
Swimming gear		
Torches		
Trainers		
Water flasks		
Wellingtons		
Wet weather gear		

	To find / buy	Got it
Entertainment – in a car & for rainy days		
Activity book e.g., word search, puzzle book		
Crayons, pens and paper		
Electronic audio equipment [3]		
Handheld consoles and chargers		
Magnetic board games: Monopoly etc.		
Stories on cassettes, CDs, DVDs, iPad		
On a plane		
Ear plugs specially designed for children		
Favourite toys, books, stickers and travel games		
Headphones		
Own food [6]		

14 - Parents and School-Aged Children

	To find / buy	Got it
On the beach		
Bat and ball		
Beach ball, large inflatable		
Beach paddle bats with balls		
Beach mats		
Beach shoes e.g., Jelly shoes		
Beach towels		
Beach toys		
Boogie board		
Bucket and spade		
Flip flops		
Football		
Kid's sun block [7]		
Sunshade		
Surfboard		
Wetsuits		

	To find / buy	Got it

#	USEFUL HINTS AND TIPS
1	**Car seat** If flying and hiring a car, you may need to check whether seats should be forward or rear-facing.
2	**Eating utensils** Soft spoons, cutlery, plates, bowls, sippy cups etc.
3	**Electronic audio equipment** CDs, iPods, handheld console, tablet, for long car journeys.
4	**Portable booster seat** Type of highchair
5	**Rucksack** Their own small one which they are responsible for, one for each child to have their own beach equipment etc. in it. Could contain: • Cap or raincoat • Own drinking flask • Trainers • Wellington or walking boots Their own personal games and other possessions

6   **Own food**

Airlines may provide children's meals or offer to heat a jar for babies, but it's best to pack a suitable snack which they will like.

Rice cakes and other healthy snacks such as fruit are the best sort of items to take.

7   **Kid's sun block**

Lotion or spray, minimum sun protection factor SPF 25 or higher.

Traveling with Pets

These days, owners of all kinds of pets are weighing up the rising cost of kennels, catteries or other forms of animal care, and deciding instead to take the dog, the cat or the budgie away with them when they go on holiday – even, in some cases, when they go abroad, especially if it's for a long period. Their reasoning is that pets – especially dogs – are stimulated by all the interesting new sights and smells. And most animals, it is thought, prefer to be with their owners rather than in the unfamiliar surroundings of the kennel or cattery. There are a number of preparatory tasks before you go however.

Our two cats frequently accompany us on holidays in the UK. We have made a very comfortable 'two-storey room' for them; a cage that sits on the folded-down back seats of our hatchback car. And there's still plenty of room in the boot!

15 - Traveling with Pets

	To find / buy	Got it
General preparation		
Find out contact details of a local vet in case of an emergency		
Foam hand cleaner		
Going abroad [1]		
Blood test certificate [1]		
EU pet passport [1]		
Insurance certificate [2]		
Medications (if any)		
Microchip certificate		
New identity tag for holiday address		
Poop scoops and po op bags		
Ticks and tapeworm prevention [3]		
Travel sickness remedy		
Vaccination certificates (rabies) [1] & [4]		

	To find / buy	Got it
Budgies and other birds		
Cage		
Cage cover		
Nuts		
Water container		
Bird food		
Wash bottle to spray their feathers with water		
Dogs		
Basket or bed		
Bath shampoo		
Blanket, favourite one		
Bowl for food		
Bowl for water		
Bowl, with lid		
Brush		
Cold weather booties, snow boots		
Cold weather jacket / coat		
Disposable bags for collecting poop		

	To find / buy	Got it
Disposable toilet gloves		
Food		
Harness		
Lead: one short and one long retractable		
Muzzle		
Paper towels		
Safety harness for car		
Spare collar with name tag and mobile number		
Travel aid – Ask your vet about DAP (Dog Appeasing Pheromone), which is also sprayed on their basket, or you can buy a collar containing DAP.		

	To find / buy	Got it
Cats		
Brush		
Collar and spare, with name tag and mobile number		
Disposable gloves		
Food		
Food bowl		
Lead: one short and one long retractable		
Litter box and litter, plastic shovel		
Paper towels		
Toys		
Travel basket or bed		
Travelling cage		
Travel aids – Feliway® (5)		
Water bowl		

#	USEFUL HINTS AND TIPS
1	When going abroad with your pet, you must take: Vaccination certificates (rabies)
	Blood test certificate
	EU pet passport – see Government website – www.gov.uk/guidance/pet-travel-to-europe-from-1-january-2021
	Port inspection by a vet for rabies on returning to the UK may require you to give the port 24 to 48 hours' notice so book an appointment unless you are coming into a large port with a resident vet.
2	**Insurance certificate** Check if your pet insurance will be valid at the location to which you are travelling, whether abroad or at home because sometimes insurance is only valid as long as the animal remains in its home territory. This is usually the case with cats.
3	**Ticks and tapeworm prevention** Ticks: you can buy a tool for removing ticks from most pet shops. Do not use alcohol to attempt to knock out the tick as this does not always work and can leave the tick's head inside the cat.

4   Vaccination certificates

For going overseas, the pet must have a rabies vaccination at least every three months and a blood test after 30 days to prove it has worked. The pet still cannot travel until six months after a negative blood test.

5   Travel aids

Cats are notorious for not liking to travel, and although most settle down after a while, there are some who will just meow all the time. Ask your vet about the product called Feliway®. This can be sprayed around the travel basket and will help soothe them.

"ARE YOU SURE THIS IS THE RIGHT PLACE?"

Adventure Holidays

This packing list is intended to cover the essentials for a variety of adventure activities from mountain walking to canal boat cruising – any holiday, in fact, that involves more active enjoyment than simply soaking up the sun. These are the kind of holidays that often mean self-catering, travelling light – maybe with just a rucksack – and camping out or staying in rough or makeshift accommodation overnight.

It was common at one time to refer to such holidays, rather disparagingly, as 'roughing it'. Indeed, they often were. As a youngster I spent many weekends as a Queen's Scout and completing my Duke of Edinburgh's Awards, clambering about with a compass, cooking on campfires and sleeping under canvas. It was great fun. Today, 'adventure' holidays for adults are far more sophisticated, made easier and more comfortable by a whole range of brilliantly designed equipment and travel companies offering to help with luggage. But whether you're hiking, canoeing, mountain biking, horse riding, rock-climbing, pony-trekking or cruising down a canal on a long boat, my lists include many essentials, along with some items you might not have thought of that will ease the organisation of 'adventure' travel.

	To find / buy	Got it
All the items in the list for Walking Holidays		
Air mats (and repair kit) or foam sleeping mat with good thermal insulation properties		
Brewing kit for a cup of tea and / or coffee		
Campsite book (if available)		
Cleaning supplies e.g., washing up liquid, dustpan and brush		
Condiments and sauces		
Cooking utensils		
Cutlery		
Dishwashing materials e.g., bowl		
Food		
Hammock and sewn-in flysheet tent		
Large mugs – unbreakable		
Pillows, inflatable		
Plastic plates and bowls for eating		
Sleeping bag liner		
Sleeping bags		
Soap and scrub brush		
Stove fuel, gas cans or solid fuel, but only if staying in the UK as they cannot be taken on a plane.		
Tent and insulating ground sheet [1]		
Tent repair kit, small one		
Thermal blanket		

	To find / buy	Got it
Toilet paper		
Toiletries		
Water filter and / or purifier combined / or water purification tablets		
Zip lock bags		

	To find / buy	Got it
Additional equipment for canoeing (check beforehand with the hire company whether you need to take these items)		
Emergency repair kit for canoe (if not supplied by canoe owner)		
Large polythene bags (for double wrapping everything if transporting your stuff)		
Lifejacket (if not supplied by canoeing holiday company)		
Water sport safety helmet (one which lets the water out) if not supplied		
Additional equipment for horse riding		
Boots for riding and long socks		
Gloves, thin, not bulky thermal, for control of reins		
Riding hat (often supplied by hiring stables)		
Riding trousers (comfortable and stretchy kind, not jeans)		

#	USEFUL HINTS AND TIPS
1	**Tent and insulating ground sheet**
	It is best if the ground sheet is sewn in or buy a modern tent with one attached. Consider a fly sheet if the weather is likely to be windy and rainy.

*Sorry, you're one sock over the
Backpacker's carry-on allowance*

Backpacking

The whole point of backpacking is that it shouldn't be backbreaking. So, the key is to start out with the bare minimum, since there are likely to be plenty of occasions when you're stuck without transport, and you'll regret every unnecessary ounce you're carrying.

In fact, you'll find that you'll be able to buy practically everything you need at almost any location on your way round the world; and you'll often be able to purchase familiar or similar products for a lot less than you would at home.

If travelling with a partner, work out beforehand what you can split between you, and share the load accordingly. And, remember you're setting out on an active holiday, so you will be roughing it for most of the time.

	To find / buy	Got it
Alarm clock, small – I have had a Westclox® Travelmate folding alarm clock for years, batteries last for a year at least.		
Bathroom wash bag with toiletries (see List 08)		
Bum bag / money bag [1]		
Camera, digital		
Compass		
Driver's Licence, UK and International [2]		
First aid kit (see List 09)		
Fleeces or woollen jumpers for cold environments/nights		
Flip flops / jelly shoes [3]		
Gaffer tape / duct tape, small roll		
Guidebooks [4]		
Hiking mattresses or ground mat for sleeping on		
Jeans, lightweight or trekking trousers with pockets, strong pairs		
Light cotton dress / sarong / pareo (for hot weather holidays)		
Long-sleeved tops		
Maps and map bag, plastic, zipped with lanyard		
Mess kit and cutlery		
Mugs, steel / enamel		
Multi-purpose Swiss Army type knife		
Pack of cards, dice or some other type of entertainment		

	To find / buy	Got it
Padlock – combination type and chain (5)		
Passport photographs, spare for passes, visas / visa extensions / student ID card		
Photocopies of documents (2)		
Photos of your family and home		
Poncho (optional)		
Rucksack		
Sandals		
Sewing kit		
Shaving kit		
Shoes such as trainers		
Shorts (6)		
Sleeping bag and sleeping sheet / sack		
Small plastic mirror		
Socks, three or four pairs, woollen, double lined for walking		
Sun hats or warm winter headgear		
Sun protection cream or spray		
Sunglasses (with straps)		
Swimwear (7)		
Tee-shirts		
Torches (8) and batteries		
Towels – light, microfibre, one large and one small		
Travel pillow		
Trousers, lightweight		
T-shirts, or similar, 2 maximum		

	To find / buy	Got it
Umbrella, compact, for sun and rain protection		
Underwear [9]		
Vaccination certificates		
Walking boots or shoes		
Walking sticks / poles (collapsible preferably)		
Washing detergent		
Water bottles, lightweight		
Water purification tablets		
Waterproof raincoat / cagoule, lightweight, foldaway		
Whistle		
World band radios [10]		
Wristwatch, a cheap one		

	To find / buy	Got it

#	USEFUL HINTS AND TIPS

1 Bum / Money Belts

If taking large amounts of cash, it is best to wear money belts underneath external clothing.

2 Documents

Photocopies of everything important (passports, travel insurance, telephone numbers etc.). Leave a copy at home, on the Internet and, if possible, give a copy to your travelling partner.

International driver's licence is required, the second part of your driving licence (the paper part) is now online.

3 Flip flops

For walking to the shower / bathroom / beach.

4 Guidebooks

A combination type and chain. When travelling on trains and buses it would be wise to chain your luggage to the luggage rack.

5 Padlock

Buy these later for countries you will not get to for a while – it will be cheaper to buy there, or you may be able to swap with other travellers.

6   Shorts

Wearing shorts are more comfortable to wear but may make you look like a tourist. You could consider safari pants (trousers) in the 'zip off at the knee' style.

Consideration must be given to which country you are in, e.g., in a Muslim country women should wear a head scarf and dresses with sleeves to the elbow.

Longer shorts that come right down to the knees are more acceptable, especially in Muslim countries.

7   Swimwear

Depending on where you are, be aware of swimwear and modesty issues. Women may be less visible and safer from harassment with a full swimming costume, rather than a two-piece costume.

8   Torches

Buy a clockwork torch / battery hand-held, which converts into a head torch. If you have a Smartphone you can get the flashlight app, but the torch will be a large drain on the battery.

9   Underwear

Depending on how many days you travel at a time; three to five pairs of pants should be enough provided that you can wash them. Bras: lightweight, non-wired and coloured bras are best.

10   World band radio

This could be an expensive extra to take, but Roberts make very robust short-wave radios.

Cruises

If you've never been on a sea or river cruise before, you may be expecting to be pampered to within an inch of your life, and this is certainly the case on most luxury cruise liners. Some ships are more family fun and youth oriented, however. Nevertheless, your enjoyment of any kind of cruise holiday will be enhanced if you make the right packing decisions. Because of what's on offer on board, you may have to change three or four times a day and you don't want to be all at sea when you're all at sea, so to speak. So it's worth taking the time to research and plan what you might need to take with you. For example, the chilly fjords of Norway or the windy Atlantic seaboard are very different cruises from those in the sunny Caribbean or the tranquil waters of the Mediterranean.

Some more upmarket cruise lines have instructions for dress on special gala evenings and in certain areas of the ship, while other cruises are designed for families and are altogether less formal, leaving it to you what you wear most of the time. There may be a themed evenings requiring fancy dress but this is usually optional. They will send you information about dress requirements when you get your confirmation letter. In general, the best guide for cruise dressing is 'dress to impress'. [4]

Many cruises are considerably longer than the usual fortnight most of us normally take for our holidays, so these will need extra careful planning and forethought. If you are flying to an embarkation point (known as fly / cruises), you will have to keep within the airline's luggage allowance. If you are departing and returning to the same port in the UK, then most cruise lines do not restrict the luggage allowance, other than a maximum weight of around 20 kg per case, but you will still have to get your luggage there. Some cruise lines offer a deluxe pick-up service from door-to-door – it costs of course but it could be worth it if you intend to take a long trip.

	To find / buy	Got it
Luggage and baggage [1]		
Women's List:		
Day wear – casual and smart casual		
Assorted tops and tee-shirts		
Dresses and skirts for daytime		
Footwear – sandals, flip flops, trainers		
Gym wear / track suit for going to the spa, pool deck, climbing wall or fitness centre		
Racket / sports kit (e.g., golf, bowls, tennis, squash, badminton if available on your ship)		
Shorts (of various weights)		
Smart jeans / light trousers		
Swimwear, at least two one-piece swimsuits / bikinis		
Wrap or fleece for cooler evenings		
For formal evenings		
Jewellery in jewellery travel purse		
Dresses, evening, long for formal nights (at least 2)		
Dresses, cocktail (2 or 3)		
Evening wrap or stole		
Trouser suit		
Nails, nail varnish, varnish remover		
Make-up and self-tan (if used)		

	To find / buy	Got it
Heated rollers or straighteners		
High-heeled formal shoes		
Clutch bag		
Also useful		
Low or comfortable shoes for walking on excursions		
Jacket or long elegant cardigan		
Hat, sun (and one which cannot blow off)		
A fan (if going to the tropics)		

	To find / buy	Got it
Men's List:		
Dinner jacket (tuxedo) [2]		
Black shoes		
Black socks		
Bow ties		
Braces or belt		
Cuff links		
Cummerbunds [3] (optional)		
Dress shirts		
Gym wear		
Jacket (smart casual)		
Scarf		
Trousers, dress and informal		
Shorts and tee-shirts for shore excursions		
Ties, not business ties		
Ties, novelty, only for themed evenings		
General for all		
Bath robe, these maybe provided for certain cabins, check first		
Binoculars if you have a cabin with a balcony		
Casual bag and attire for shore trips and daytime on board		

	To find / buy	Got it
Champagne bottle corker		
Dance shoes		
Fancy dress evening outfit / mask / make-up [4]		
Novelty fridge magnets [6]		
Climbing gear: some ships have a climbing wall		
Sports gear for on-board sports e.g., golf if they have nets, table tennis		
Sports gear for on-board sports e.g., golf if they have nets, table tennis		
Goggles etc.		
Warm outer wear e.g., coat / jacket / gloves / hat (only if going to Scandinavia, Russia and / or Arctic areas)		
Sea sickness tablets (see Medical List 09)		
Theme night dress [4]		

#	USEFUL HINTS AND TIPS

1 Luggage and baggage

If you are travelling or returning to the UK by ship, then you have the advantage and luxury of unlimited baggage! Remember you still have to get it to the port.

2 Dinner jacket

Check with the itinerary for the cruise as to how many formal dress evenings there will be and take required dresses or shirts. They usually tell you this in advance – each night is designated formal or informal. You are given full instructions on how to dress if you wish to join in. If not, you could just stay in the less formal eating / pool areas or in your cabin.

If you have not got a dinner jacket or tuxedo, then they should allow a lounge or dark suit and tie. If your weight allowance is still border line, then just take a smart pair of trousers, a coloured shirt and matching tie. You could travel out in the trousers.

3 Cummerbunds

For strict adherence to dress rules, the bow tie colour should be the same colour as the cummerbund. (Cummerbunds used to be instead of pockets, so the leaves must open upwards.)

As a nice touch, the colour of the bow tie and cummerbund could match the prominent colour of a partner's evening dress.

Novelty bow ties are definitely out (unless needed for the themed night). The only acceptable colours for bow ties are black, white, blue and red (maybe gold or silver).

4   Theme night dress

Check with the itinerary for the cruise for the fancy dress evening theme.

These could be

70s, 80s, 90s

Caribbean

Circus

Cops and Robbers

Cowboys and Indians

Fairy-tale

Gala night, there may be more than one

Gangsters

Hawaiian

Mediterranean

Neon

Officers and Gentlemen

Pirates

Uniforms

Venetian Masques

White night

5   Check the excursion itinerary of the ports for the clothes you may need. For example, on some cruises they may have a tour on horse-back or a ramble across hillsides, so you may want to take appropriate clothing.

6   Useful Extras

Novelty fridge magnets. All cabin doors are steel and as you cannot send a text message to someone on board, you can leave messages for friends / family on your door or on their cabin door.

Glastonbury

If this is your first trip as a festival goer, then you are in for a lot of fun, but there are pitfalls a-plenty. This list is designed to help you avoid them, and to have the best time possible.

Going to a festival is in many ways very similar to a camping holiday, so you can cross-reference this list with the Camping List to make doubly sure you don't forget anything.

Of course, the mud and other inconveniences of a festival campsite are not for everyone. Glamping is your alternative, and the list also includes pointers for staying at a nearby hotel, hostel, or B & B.

The main thing to remember about going to a festival is that you are attending a celebration of music and culture. The core audience for many of these events are younger people but a lot of festivals, including Glastonbury, WOMAD and Latitude, also have attendees of all ages, and no one need feel out of place. As long as you go prepared, you are in for an unforgettable experience...

Remember, pack light, you are not going on a cruise for three weeks!

19 - Glastonbury

	To find / buy	Got it
Boots [1]		
Baby wipes		
Cereal Bars [2]		
Ear plugs		
Fairy Lights [3]		
Foldaway chair / shooting stick seat		
Glitter [4]		
Hand mirror		
Hand sanitiser		
Head torch		
Night mask		
Pop-up tent		
Portable phone charger (Juice box) [5]		
Pro Plus		
Refillable water bottle		
Sack trolley [6]		
She-Wee		
Small rucksack		
Sunglasses		
Suntan lotion		
Tent – pop-up [7]		
Tarpaulin [8]		
Toilet paper		
Tutus [4]		
Warm clothes for evening		

The author allows this check page to be photocopied when packing for your current holiday

	To find / buy	Got it
Waterproof jacket		
Wellington long socks		
Wellingtons – Yellow		
Wigs [4]		

#	USEFUL HINTS AND TIPS

1   **Boots**

Go in a good pair of walking / hiking shoes. You will be doing a lot of walking from one gig to another and not on good ground. Still have wellies as if very muddy then better than hiking shoes. Do not take sandals, maybe pair of flip flops.

2   **Cereal Bars**

Bring a family pack, needed to snack on throughout the day.

3   **Fairy Lights**

battery powered, rechargeable, on top of your tent to guide you back to your tent when it is dark.

4   **Glitter, Wigs and Tutus**

For fancy dress on the main evening.

5   **Portable phone charger (Juice box)**

Enough extra power to last at least a day

6   **Sack trolly**

Get small but with good wheels to take your suitcases, tent, bags from the car park to your tent area in one journey, as you don't want to be running back and forward to the car park.

7   Tent

Opt for a tent slightly bigger than what you actually need, a 'two-man' tent is never really spacious enough for two people.

It's also worth investing in a colourful tent or flag to ensure you can find your tent among all the others.

Do a tent 'test run' a few days before the festival in your back garden; that way you can ensure you have all the pegs and there aren't any repairs to be done.

8   Tarpaulin

This is ideal to sit on, but also to reserve a tent area next to yours for some friends.

9   Pack light, you are not going on a cruise for three weeks.

Active Holidays in the Sun

Flying off to sunnier climes demands plenty of preparation. If you simply intend to chill out, and your idea of relaxation is to sit around a pool within easy reach of a piña colada, then your basic kit will consist of a swimsuit, suntan lotion, a hat to keep the sun off the back of your neck, sunglasses and a supply of good books / magazines.

If, however, you prefer to sample the various activities on hand at most resorts these days, you may consider taking your own equipment such as tennis rackets or wet suits, surfboards or snorkelling gear. Just check in advance to compare the cost of hiring locally against the cost of transporting your own stuff because you will almost certainly have to pay extra for these if travelling by air.

This is a list of items to take for a beach / activity (sailing, tennis, water-skiing) holiday outside the UK.

And if you are looking for action after the sun goes down, don't forget to pack your dancing shoes.

20 - Active Holidays in the Sun

	To find / buy	Got it
Ant / roach spray		
Bandana / sun hat		
Beach towel and / or mat [1]		
Camera		
Clothing for cooler evenings including jacket or wrap		
Clothing for dancing / night clubs		
Cover-up from sun such as sarong / pareo		
Flip flops or jelly shoes		
Freeze spray for muscular discomfort		
Ice bag for injuries		
Insect repellent cream / spray for skin		
Lightweight jacket for cool evenings		
Medication (see Medical List 09)		
Mosquito spray / coils / plugs – if applicable		
Reading glasses		
Short-sleeved shirts		
Shorts		
Sunburn or after sun cream, aloe vera gel, moisturising creme		
Sun hat		
Sunglasses, at least two pairs		
Suntan protective lotion [2]		
Swimwear and swimming cap		
Tee-shirts, several		

	To find / buy	Got it
Activity kit		
Gloves for water-skiing and sailing		
If on a sailing holiday, take your RYA (Royal Yachting Association) book and certificates or copies of these		
Jelly shoes to wear when sailing and on the beach		
Sailing gloves		
Sandals, deck shoes		
Snorkel, flippers		
Sports kit – trainers, sweatband, wrist band, shorts, polo shirts, sports bra, socks		
Sports / sailing sunglasses with lanyard		
Swimming goggles [3]		
Table tennis bats (if not supplied)		
Tennis balls (check if they provide these)		
Tennis elbow arm band		
Tennis racket(s) and case		
Tennis shoes		
Trainers		
Wetsuit (if not available – check)		
Wristwatch, sports type with GPS navigation if possible		

#	USEFUL HINTS AND TIPS

1 Beach towel

Many hotels provide these so this may be an item you could leave out if your weight allowance is getting near to the maximum.

In case you forget to take it back to your room, put your name on it or some identification mark.

2 Suntan protective lotion

Use at least SPF (Sun Protection Factor) 25 sunblock (the minimum recommended by the Imperial Cancer Research Fund); allow at least 100 ml per day. Be generous with your application.

If going on holiday by yourself, then you could take a soft radiator brush for putting lotion on to the middle of your back.

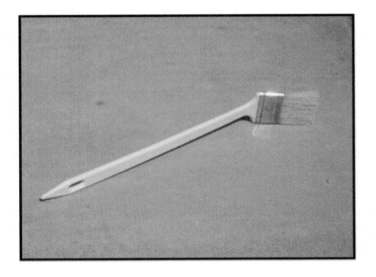

Holiday Camp
or Chalet in the UK

Britain's first holiday camp, the Cunningham Camp, was established on the Isle of Man in the 1890s. It claimed to provide 'the greatest possible amount of health and enjoyment that may be obtained for the least possible expenditure of cash' – a noble objective that made the camp incredibly successful. It also advised prospective campers that, as far as packing was concerned, 'a small Gladstone bag should hold all necessary articles'.

Today's holiday camps – even the most sophisticated – are no different from Cunningham's in the sense that they aim to remove as much of the burden of thinking about what to do and how to look after yourself as possible from customers. This is what makes them so popular with families with younger children. Such camps pride themselves in having thought of practically everything, so it's worth checking them out online or in their brochure before you pack stuff you really don't need in your Gladstone bag!

If you have stayed at the camp before, you will have some experience, which will help in tailoring this list. It can be useful to find out what you may hire at the camp e.g., toaster, microwave, iron etc., and how much it costs. A lot of camps provide the items in this list.

If you are travelling in a large group or with more than one family, establish who is bringing what before you leave to save duplication.

Food is not included on this list so, as far as you can, decide who is buying food, who is doing the cooking and who is cooking which meals before you set off. Make a separate list!

Also discuss money matters such as having a kitty for spending on food etc.

	To find / buy	Got it
Air-freshener spray for bathroom		
Aprons for each member of the family		
Bathmat		
Bedding, extra [1]		
Bottle opener		
CD player or amps for mobile phones		
Cheese grater		
Colanders		
Corkscrew		
Extension leads and adaptors, at least two or more		
Fly spray		
Games: Monopoly, Scrabble, playing cards etc.		
Green scouring pads		
Hairdryer		
Hand soap		
Hot water bottles (for autumn or winter breaks)		
Household cleaning liquid		
Iron (check if supplied)		
Mugs, as some chalets only provide tiny cups		
Paper tissues		
Paper towels		
Picnic items such as plastic plates, boxes, flasks and plastic cutlery		

	To find / buy	Got it
Pillows and cases		
Potato masher		
Potato peeler		
Radio		
Saucepans / frying pans (good quality), if serious about cooking		
Shower gel		
Sink cleaner and cloth		
Skewers		
Stain removal fluid / sachets		
Tea towels		
Toaster		
Toilet rolls		
Washing-up brush		
Washing-up gloves		
Washing-up liquid		
Waste bin liners		
Wire coat hangers (leave them behind on departure)		

21 - Holiday Camp or Chalet in the UK

	To find / buy	Got it
Extra items to take depending on the type of holiday		
Beach equipment such as mats / umbrellas / wind breaks / balls, if near to the seaside		
Dance shoes		
Football		
Golf shoes and golf clubs		
Ice skates		
Knives, favourite cooking knife		
Riding outfit: boots, hat, gloves		
Roller skates		
Rucksacks		
Sailing gear		
Spa wear such as track suit and flip flops		
Swimsuits and large towels		
Walking boots or shoes		

#	USEFUL HINTS AND TIPS
1	**Bedding** Extra winter bedding, extra blankets, a spare duvet or sleeping bag, or an electric blanket, depending on the time of year and your past experience of chalet camps.
2	Get to the camp early as you can, so you are not carrying bags a long way.

Rain Forest / Jungle Trips

Of all the trips in the Holiday Packing Guide, this is the one where you're most likely to find yourself in completely alien surroundings, remote from the familiar comforts of civilisation, so planning what you take with you is essential.

Assuming you're going on an organised expedition in a group – and I most certainly don't advise you to go blundering off into the rainforest on your own – your guide or holiday company will, of course, let you know about any special gear you should equip yourself with.

Be warned: it doesn't matter how many TV documentaries you've seen or how many times you've been to the Eden Project, if this is your first time in jungle conditions, nothing will have prepared you for the extremes of temperature and humidity you'll encounter. And you'll attract the interest of all sorts of exotic insects and other creatures you might prefer to keep at arm's length. So this list includes a number of clothing and insect repellent items that are absolute musts.

22 - Rain Forest / Jungle Trips

	To find / buy	Got it
Anti-malaria tablets, see Medical List 11		
Binoculars [1]		
Camera [2]		
Compass		
Documents [3]		
Hammock and sewn-in flysheet tent		
Insect repellent [4]		
Iodine or purifying tablets for water sterilisation (see Medical List 09 for further information)		
Jeans or, better still, trousers, lightweight, combat type that dry very quickly [5]		
Kit bag/day sack/backpack [6]		
Knife, multi-purpose [7]		
Light cotton dresses / sarong		
Lip balm / sun protection		
Moisturiser		
Money belt, a waterproof one for swimming is useful		
Mosquito net, travel kind, impregnated with insecticide		
Poncho or cagoule (lightweight, waterproof) [8]		
Prescription glasses, if needed [9]		
Sealable, zipped bags for documents / maps on a neck strap		
Shirts		
Sun hat [10]		

The author allows this check page to be photocopied when packing for your current holiday

	To find / buy	Got it
Sun protection cream / lotion		
Sunglasses		
Swimsuits		
Tee-shirts, short- and long-sleeved		
Thermal water bottle		
Torch and batteries or clockwork torch		
Towels, if required, microfibre for carrying		
Walking or hiking boots or shoes [11]		
Water-free wash [12]		
Waterproof jacket (nylon) that folds up into a small bag [13]		
Whistle		

	To find / buy	Got it

#	USEFUL HINTS AND TIPS

1 **Binoculars**

6 x 40 recommended. Those that are any more powerful than 6 magnifications will be hard to hold in a moving vehicle, as they will be bigger and heavier.

2 **Camera**

If you have a SLR camera, then take at least a 300mm zoom lens for close-ups.

Memory cards: buy the largest one you can afford. You can delete unwanted images from your camera later in the holiday.

3 **Documents**

Any paper items must be kept in a sealed bag in high humidity otherwise they will get damp and the pages will stick together.

It may be difficult to find a shop with cards and stamps, let alone a post box. In the big towns you can post items at the mail centres.

4 **Insect repellent**

Get one that is 50% DEET. NB only 20% DEET should be used on children.

DEET (chemical name, Diethyltoluamide) is the active ingredient in many insect repellent products. It is used to repel biting pests such as mosquitoes and ticks, including ticks that may carry Lyme disease, Deng fever, Yellow fever.

DEET is designed for direct application to human skin and will repel insects, rather than kill them.

| 5 | **Trousers** |

Combat type, light 100% cotton, not denim as it can be hot, restrict movement, and when wet takes too long to dry out. When viewing game or hiking, white is not a suitable colour. It increases your visibility to the animals and will also get dirty quickly.

Shorts

Although shorts are cooler, long trousers will protect your legs from bites, grazes / scratches from the bush and scrub etc. You could consider the type of safari pants (trousers) which 'zip off at the knee'. These are good for wearing as shorts during the day and as long trousers at dusk when the mosquitoes start biting.

Do not wear camouflage material, for the obvious reason that in many places it symbolises the army.

It is best to pack durable but light clothing. This will be cooler to wear and easier to wash and dry.

| 6 | **Kit bag / small backpack / day sack / small rucksack / fanny pack or bum bag** |

For excursions / day trips to carry water, money, camera equipment, notebook etc.

| 7 | **Knife** |

Multi-purpose (e.g., Gerber®, Victorinox®, and Leatherman®) is useful – but do not take any knives onto a plane, even a small key ring knife.

| 8 | **Poncho or cagoule** |

Take a waterproof, not woollen or cotton, poncho suitable for the tropical heavy rainfall that you will experience.

9   Glasses, prescription (if you wear them)

It will be very dusty and contact lenses may not be suitable. Take lens wipes.

10   Sun hat

It is best to have a large peak on a baseball cap, but better still is a large brimmed hat which also protects the back of your neck. Some have a flap of material at the back for this.

11   Walking or hiking boots or shoes

To save valuable weight and space, you could travel out in these. Just remember that some airports will ask you to take boots off for inspection.

Your boots should be of the waterproof, Gore-Tex®, Sympatex® type, with a good gripping sole, and, above all, keep your feet warm and dry.

12   Water-free wash

Water-free wash or alcohol gel to clean hands after going to the toilet.

13   Waterproof jacket and trousers

Those that are Gore-Tex®, Sympatex® type are best.

"I TOLD YOU WE SHOULD'VE TAKEN THE BALLOON TRIP!"

Safari Holidays

For many people, the prime reason for going on a safari holiday is to see and record the stunning scenery and exotic wildlife in its natural habitat. So at the top of your list should be a good pair of binoculars and a decent camera (with plenty of memory space if it's digital) with a good zoom lens.

Most safari organisers will provide you with a list of essential items you should take with you, as well as information regarding any jabs you should get. One piece of valuable advice is to take neutral coloured clothing – that is, avoid bright colours or white shirts when on the trail, because you need to merge with the landscape and fit in with the wildlife as much as possible.

Safari holidays usually involve sleeping in a tent at least part of the time, often with limited or no washing facilities, so you may as well resign yourself to the fact that you won't look your best. Pack with this in mind.

	To find / buy	Got it
Binoculars [1]		
Camera [2]		
Clothes: cotton blouses, shirts, long-sleeved		
Cotton jeans or safari trousers for evenings		
Jacket, warm and wind / showerproof, which will fold up into a small bag		
Trousers and jeans which are lightweight, may be combat type [3]		
Light cotton dress / sarong / pareo		
Smart / casual trousers for evenings [3]		
Sweater or fleece for cooler evenings [4]		
Glasses, prescription [5]		
Insect repellent [6]		
Kit bag / day sack / backpack [7]		
Knife, multi-purpose, Swiss army type [8]		
Money belt, a waterproof one can be useful		
Sleeping bag and small pillow (warm sleeping bag or blanket for winter trips)		
Small handbag		
Sun hat [9]		
Sunglasses		
Sun protection lotion		

	To find / buy	Got it
Swimsuit		
Thermal water bottle		
Torch and batteries or clockwork torch		
Towels, if required		
Underwear, socks and tee-shirts		
Walking shoes or hiking boots [10]		
Water-free wash [11]		

23 - Safari Holidays

	To find / buy	Got it
Essential personal / medical items		
After sun treatment such as aloe vera gel		
An assortment of sticking plasters		
Anti-diarrhoea pills and laxatives		
Anti-malaria tablets (see your doctor about this beforehand)		
Antiseptic cream		
Deodorant		
Eye drops		
Insect bite relief cream		
Insect repellent cream or spray		
Lip balm		
Moisturiser		
Rehydration powder / sachets		

3 - Safari Holidays

#	USEFUL HINTS AND TIPS
1	**Binoculars**

6 x 40 recommended. Any more powerful than x 6 magnifications will be hard to hold steady in a moving vehicle.

| 2 | **Camera** |

If you have a SLR camera, then take at least a 75 - 300mm zoom lens for close-ups.

Memory Cards – buy the largest one you can afford. You can delete any unwanted images from your digital camera later in the trip.

| 3 | **Jeans / trousers** |

Combat type, light 100% cotton, not denim as it is heavy, restricts movement and takes too long to dry out. When viewing game or hiking, white is not a suitable colour. It increases your visibility to the animals and will also get dirty quickly.

Shorts

Shorts are cooler but long trousers will protect your legs from bites / grazes / scratches from the bush and scrub etc.

You could consider the type of safari pants (trousers) that 'zip off at the knee'. These are good for wearing as shorts during the day and as long trousers at dusk when the mosquitoes start biting.

All clothes should be 100% cotton.

Do not wear camouflage material: in many places it symbolises the army.

It is best to pack durable but light clothing. This will be cooler to wear and easier to wash and dry.

4   **Fleece, jumper, jersey**

Layers are most practical; it will be cold in the mornings and evenings when going out and coming back on game drives, but hot during the day.

Take a warm jacket if travelling in colder climates. Check what season you are travelling out to.

5   **Glasses, prescription (if worn)**

It will be very dusty and contact lenses may not be suitable. Lens wipes would be useful.

6   **Insect repellent**

Get 50% DEET. NB only 20% DEET can be used on children.

DEET (chemical name, Diethyltoluamide) is the active ingredient in many insect repellent products. It is used to repel biting pests such as mosquitoes and ticks, including ticks that may carry Lyme disease etc.

DEET is designed for direct application to human skin and will repel insects, rather than kill them.

7   **Kit bag / small backpack / day sack / small rucksack / fanny pack or bum bag**

For excursions / day trips to carry water, money, camera equipment, notebook etc.

8   **Knife**

Multi-purpose, Swiss army type (e.g., Gerber®, Victorinox®, Leatherman®) – do not take any knives on to a plane, even a small key ring knife.

9	**Sun hat**
	best to have a large peak, but better still is a rimmed one that also protects the back of your neck.
10	**Walking shoes or hiking boots**
	Trainers are not suitable for safari hikes as your feet will sweat a lot and feel uncomfortable.
11	**Water-free wash**
	Water-free wash or alcohol gel to clean hands after going to the toilet.

Other points to be aware of:

1.	Check the tours on the itinerary. For example, they may have a horseback tour, so you may want to take your riding hat, boots and jodhpurs (unless they provide these at the venue), or maybe you will need your walking boots, poles, etc.
2.	If camping, then do not take food / drink into the sleeping tents as this encourages animals to come in. Also try to keep toiletries away from the sleeping tents – hyenas eat soap!
3.	It's worth checking what you'll need with most tour operators who will give you help and advice before you go.

Sailing on a Yacht

There's sailing and there's sailing.

At one end of the spectrum there's having serious fun in sailing dinghies on lakes or just off the seashore. At the other end, there's open sea yachting, where you play your part as a member of a highly proficient crew sailing at speed from one place to another.

If you're a regular sailor of the latter type, you'll know that storage is at a premium on yachts, so it's a good idea to pack a medium-sized soft bag or case that will make it easier to stow below.

When going on holiday, whether you're sailing an ocean-going yacht or simply messing about in boats, you'll find essential safety equipment (lifejackets, smocks, waterproofs etc.) will normally be provided. However, you may want to take your own but if you do, always check that everything is still in good condition. A lifejacket should be serviced every two years and some items may need replacing such as CO_2 cylinders, automatic cartridges or water-soluble bobbins, retaining clips etc. Check the lifejackets bought for your children, who may have outgrown theirs.

	To find / buy	Got it
After sun moisturising cream / Aloe Vera gel		
Bean bag, small, for balancing camera on Land Rover roof		
Binoculars [1]		
Buoyancy aid / lifejacket (make sure it's serviced and the right size for children)		
Camera – waterproof one is best		
Clothing and shoes for general onshore wear		
Cruiser / sailing wear		
Deck shoes, flat non-slip sandals [2]		
Fishing equipment (optional)		
Gaffer tape / duct tape, small roll.		
Gloves, sailing gloves (short-fingered)		
Insect repellent		
Jelly shoes		
Knife, sailing knife (stainless steel) – multi-purpose [3]		
Medication (if used)		
Mosquito cream / coils / plugs – if applicable		
Padlock – combination type		
Rash vest		
Reading glasses / case if required		
Royal Yachting Association (RYA) book and certificates or copies of these		
Safety harness (maybe supplied – check)		

The author allows this check page to be photocopied when packing for your current holiday

	To find / buy	Got it
Safety pins [4]		
Seasickness pills		
Shorts		
Smocks, waterproof		
Snorkel, flippers, weight belt		
Sun cap with strap and clip on to shirt		
Sun hat, baseball cap		
Sunglasses floaters and straps		
Sunglasses, 2 pairs [5]		
Sun protection lotion		
Suitcase / bag – must be a soft one for easy storage on the yacht		
Swimsuit		
Thermals (if sailing in cold conditions)		
Towel, small, quick drying		
Wetsuit		
Wristwatch – sports type		

24 - Sailing on a Yacht

	To find / buy	Got it

The author allows this check page to be photocopied when packing for your current holiday

#	USEFUL HINTS AND TIPS
1	**Binoculars**
	6 x 40 are recommended. Any more powerful than 6 magnifications will be hard to hold in a moving vessel, as they will be bigger and heavier.
2	**Deck shoes / sandals**
	Soft, non-slip, non-marking for all footwear.
3	**Knife**
	Multi-purpose Swiss army type. (e.g., Gerber® or Victorinox®, Leatherman®) – do not take any knives onto a plane, even a small key ring knife.
4	**Safety pins**
	To attach your washing to the washing line so if they come off the line they don't blow overboard!
5	**Sunglasses**
	When sailing on a yacht, Polaroid are the best type of sunglasses as they reduce glare and allow you to see through the reflective surface of the water.

Skiing Holidays

The kind of skiing equipment you need can vary greatly according to your degree of proficiency but whether you're a novice or a seasoned skier, it can be hired at most resorts. For instance, ski boots have improved immensely in recent years, and it's now very easy for a beginner to hire a well-fitting pair. Some hire shops will sell you the boots you hired for your holiday if you find them comfortable, which can save money in the long run. It is certainly worthwhile if you've caught the skiing bug and intend to come back year after year.

To hire or buy your skis is more of a personal preference. I'm a keen skier, but I still prefer to hire them. The disadvantages of having your own pair are: they cost a lot; they are difficult (and expensive) to travel with; they're easily damaged and just as easily stolen. Besides, as your skill improves, you can swap your first basic hire skis for a higher-grade pair during the course of your holiday or later on as time goes by.

Just as essential as skis and boots are your gloves and sunglasses or ski mask. Gloves should be leather or similar material so if someone skies over your hand it will not take all the skin off. Sunglasses / ski masks are best bought at the resort, as you will need a good pair of Cat 2 glasses (middle quality). These are not always available in shops in the UK. Ski masks are best for children as they cannot lose them.

Buy the Ski Tracks app, or similar one for your smart phone. It's good to see how much skiing you have done at the end of the day.

	To find / buy	Got it
Clothes for evenings		
Down-filled jacket [1]		
Ear warmers / muffs		
Gaffer / duck-tape, red or other bright colour to put on hire skies to easily identify them, and maybe stop someone taking them by mistake		
Gloves / mittens, both short and gauntlet length, no need for casual ones		
Gloves, thin ones to double up inside gauntlets		
Hand-warmers [2]		
Hat, both woolly and casual one		
Headband, woolly		
Helmet and liner		
Hip flask or ski poles which can contain drinking liquids		
Leg supports (if worried about an old injury)		
Lip protection cream / Vaseline		
Map / piste map / guidebook		
Mobile hands-free kit		
Mobile phone [3]		
Neck gaiter or scarf		
Skis [4]		
Ski backpack		
Ski boots and bag suitable to go as luggage		

	To find / buy	Got it
Ski clips / ties, Velcro tape		
Ski lock for padlocking skis and padlock for ski locker		
Ski mask or goggles		
Ski shirts, thick type with chest pockets, 100% cotton: travel out in one		
Ski socks		
Ski suit, jacket, pants, vest, fleece		
Skis, poles and bag – if taking them with you. Book them in on the plane / train		
Slippers [5]		
Snacks for instant energy e.g., Kendal mint cake, chocolate, nut bars etc.		
Snowshoes [6]		
Sunglasses cord retainer (or frame sides which curl around your ears)		
Sunglasses, ski, wrap-around type [7]		
Sun protection lotion, small size when skiing [8], see Medical Items list		
Ski socks		
Thermal underwear (long-sleeved crewneck and long johns)		
Turtlenecks / polar buffs		
Two-way radios (Walkie talkies) if you are with someone or in a party		
Warm clothing (merino wool is the warmest)		
Wax for skis		
Whistle [9]		

#	USEFUL HINTS AND TIPS

1   **Down-filled jacket**

Your ski jacket will also be your general jacket for wearing off the slopes. If you are at the limit for airline weight allowance, then don't pack it; travel out in it.

2   **Hand-warmers**

Take two double packs of reusable hand-warmers.

3   **Mobile phone**

Key the SOS (Save Our Souls) number taken from the piste map into the memory before you set out on the first day.

4   **Skis**

If hiring equipment, make sure you know your weight in all your kit, boots included and your height in centimetres.

5   **Slippers**

To wear around the hotel or maybe on a long-haul fight.

6   **Snowshoes / boots**

To save valuable weight and space, you could travel out in these. Just remember that some airports will ask you to take boots off for inspection. Your snow boots should be of the waterproof, Gore-Tex®, Sympatex® type, with a good gripping sole, and, above all, keep your feet warm and dry.

7   Sunglasses

Ski wrap-around type are best to prevent the side burn from glare damaging your eyes. These could have interchangeable lenses such as blue / grey for bright sun, orange for poor light, yellow for flat light etc.

They need to have a high UV number to protect your eyes.

8   Sun protection lotion

Take a large bottle of SPF 50 and apply to all of your face and neck at the beginning of every day. Be more careful of the sun late in the season, April – May as the sun is very strong. Apply at every coffee stop you have.

The ultimate protection is a paste which I have only been able to buy in France called is 8882 Crème Labial 'H' Haute Protection SPF 50. This will stop any sun getting to your skin, best on end of nose and lips.

9   Whistle

For emergency use. Blow six short blasts, repeated at regular intervals, if you require aid on the slopes.

Walking Holidays in the UK

The UK has become one of the most walker-friendly nations in the world. From gentle coastal routes to Snowdonia, from moors to fells, from Hadrian's Wall to the Pennine Way, the number of possible walks that criss-cross and encircle Britain is enormous; equally remarkable is the variety of stunning landscapes walkers can enjoy. So popular have walking vacations become that there are now dedicated dog-walking holidays!

The following list is for those who belong to that growing band of all ages who have a liking for hiking. It really is worth taking the trouble to equip yourself appropriately, whether you're tackling the mighty Helvellyn mountain in the Eastern Fells or taking an afternoon stroll along a section of The Ridgeway in Wiltshire; you'll always enjoy your walking more if you're comfortably attired and properly provisioned.

Whether your holiday involves overnight stays at Youth Hostels, B&Bs or luxury hotels, the list overleaf is designed to help you on your way. Before leaving for any walking holiday, check websites for the latest information on the location, weather, trail conditions, etc.

	To find / buy	Got it
Personal items		
Blister treatment		
Boots [1]		
Fleeces or jumpers		
Gaiters (optional)		
Gloves		
Hat, maybe one with peak (baseball hat)		
Jacket, waterproof [2]		
Jacket: under jacket, filled with down (for colder months)		
Mobile phone		
Multi-purpose knife, Swiss army type (e.g., Gerber®, Victorinox®, Leatherman®)		
Passport-size photographs for passes etc.		
Permits and entry passes		
Poncho or cagoule, waterproof		
Scarf		
Several pairs of thick socks		
Shaving gear		
Shorts (for summer months)		
Sunglasses		
Thermal underwear (for colder months)		
Toiletries and wash bags		
Trousers, light, wind-proof (not denim jeans)		
Trousers, waterproof [2]		
Turtleneck tops		

The author allows this check page to be photocopied when packing for your current holiday

	To find / buy	Got it
Walking stick / poles (collapsible)		
Water bottle / carrier bag		
Equipment		
App for an altimeter for your smart phone		
Binoculars, 6 x 40 will be a good size, unless you are bird spotting.		
Camera		
Compass		
Emergency bivouac bag		
First aid kit. See List 09		
Guidebooks		
Insect repellent		
Lighter / matches		

	To find / buy	Got it
Maps in water-resistant plastic case on a lanyard		
Membership cards [3]		
Mirror, unbreakable, polished, stainless steel or plastic		
Radio for weather reports [4]		
Rucksack or bum bag / fanny pack		
Sunburn treatment cream / gel		
Sun protection cream / lotion		
Survival bag, thermal blanket		
Torch, battery or wind-up		
Two-way radios (Walkie-talkies) if you are with someone else or in a party, or you could have an app on your smart phone.		
Whistle [4]		

	To find / buy	Got it

#	USEFUL HINTS AND TIPS

1 **Boots**

Walking boots or shoes must be comfortable and worn in. They should be waterproof, Gore-Tex®, Sympatex® type, have a good grip and keep your feet warm and dry.

2 **Waterproof jacket / trousers**

Waterproof and windproof jacket and shower-proof trousers: Gore-Tex®, Sympatex® type. Denim jeans should never be worn for walking as they restrict your movement when wet, are not warm enough in cold weather and take a long time to dry.

Points to consider when buying new waterproofs. SympaTex is more comfortable to wear than Gore-Tex as it has the ability to stretch more, which is what you need when walking, especially for leggings. Gore-Tex does not stretch as much and is a bit stiffer.

3   Membership cards
Websites for walking in the UK.

National Trails: www.nationaltrail.co.uk

National Trust: www.nationaltrust.org.uk

English Heritage: www.english-heritage.org.uk

Ramblers Association: www.ramblers.org.uk

YHA (Youth Hostel Association): www.yha.org.uk

Scotland: www.syha.org.uk

4   Whistle
For emergency use. Blow six short blasts, repeated at regular intervals if you require aid or assistance.

Weekend / City Breaks

There's an art to travelling light. It's almost a state of mind – a way of thinking as well as a way of packing.

Before you decide on what clothes to take on your short break, stop, think, and make a few reasonable guesses. What kind of weather can you expect? How much time will you spend outside? What kind of social situations / occasions will you find yourself in? Can you go without shaving for a few days, and will anybody mind if you do? Will you really need to wash your hair while you're away for a couple of days – and even if you do, do you actually need to take your own hairdryer and heated rollers?

Here's another useful tip: ignore the local temperature while you're packing. If it's cold and grey outside, you'll be tempted to put in a jumper you may not need; or if the sun's hot, you'll probably pack something far too light!

Just remember: the reason for taking a weekend or city break – whether you're staying with friends, using a B&B or booking into a hotel – is to get away from your usual environment and relax. You may also enjoy new experiences and see lots of interesting art and architecture. The list compiled overleaf is designed to help you stick to the basics.

	To find / buy	Got it
Bathroom toiletry bag – see Toiletry Bathroom bag List 10 for contents		
Clothes – enough for 3 or 4 days, suitable for the season		
Coat or jacket (suitable for the weather conditions)		
Ear plugs or headphones		
Eye mask (if you have trouble sleeping)		
Hat and gloves (depending on the season)		
Medication, see Medical List 09		
Notebook and pen / book		
Paper tissues and hand cleanser		
Pillowcases (optional) [1]		
Rucksack, backpack or bum bag / handbag		
Shoes – a stout walking pair and a smarter pair for evenings		
Sleepwear		
Slippers or flip flops		
Smoke alarm [2]		
Spare car keys (if you drove to the airport / departure point)		

	To find / buy	Got it
Swimwear [3]		
Torch (small, e.g., Mini Maglite®)		
Towel, small		
Travel alarm clock (unless you have a phone alarm app)		
Umbrella, telescopic		
Underwear		

#	USEFUL HINTS AND TIPS
1	**Pillowcases**

Take an extra pillowcase(s) to put over the B&B's / hotel's pillowcase as an extra layer between their pillow and you if you are backpacking in rough areas or worried about the cleanliness of where you might stay.

2   Smoke alarm

Some B&Bs may not have the fire protection which guest houses and hotels must have. They may not even have any smoke alarms in the house, so it's a good idea to take a small domestic one, or a combination smoke and carbon monoxide detector.

3   Swimwear

If staying in a hotel by the sea or with a pool or spa centre. Check beforehand.

About the Author

To some degree, my love of list-making is reminiscent of the fictional character Brian Stimpson, played masterfully by John Cleese in the film *Clockwise*. Stimpson is a headmaster who runs – some would say ruins – every aspect of his life to the minute. It transpires that this all-consuming habit came about because he was so bad at timekeeping in his youth, and  now his pendulum has swung to the opposite extreme.

I can easily identify with Brian Stimpson. Many years ago, I noticed that every time I went on holiday, I ended up forgetting something – or, worse still, I would wish I'd packed completely differently. I should mention at this point that I have been a Quality Manager and Lead Auditor in the construction industry. For over 30 years, my working life has been concerned with checking and rechecking procedures and checklists for projects large and small. So the solution to my problem was staring me in the face: I started making holiday checklists.

For a long time, business trips had taken me to Africa and the Gulf States, during which I was lucky enough to spend many a weekend travelling in the bush or the desert. These 'work vacations' whetted my appetite and led me to explore the Far East too. So I spent many a long hour packing for many a long flight. I even lived out of a suitcase for a while, an experience I do *not* recommend!

Then there's the legacy of my youth. I don't know whether Brian Stimpson was a Scout, but I certainly was. I hiked, camped and canoed all over Britain, as well as becoming a Queen's Scout and gaining my Duke of Edinburgh's Awards. I remain a keen sportsman, skiing regularly in the Alps and taking activity holidays in various locations around Europe.

In the spirit of Brian Stimpson, I find it really satisfying to have packed for a holiday or trip, in the sure and certain knowledge that my list is checked and that I've forgotten nothing. Disorganisation no longer plagues me. And to ensure that it never will again, I keep it at bay by making notes of any changes or new items I should include, altering my main lists accordingly on my return. My lists also provide an added benefit: I can see immediately if anything has been lost or mislaid while I've been away.

Most of all, I trust *you* will gain from *my* past errors and omissions!

I hope you will enjoy using my lists and will add to or adapt them where you see fit.

Andy Hind
January 2022

Acknowledgments

As the author of this book, I would like to acknowledge my gratitude for the help I received in preparing this book. My thanks go to all those individuals for their support, advice and encouragement.

The following people were invaluable in the process of producing this book and I am especially grateful for their help.

Alexandra Arlango
Becki Davis
Christine Davis
Elizabeth Arlango
My Mum, Iris

And also

Carol Hatton	Ian Smith
Catherine Jarvie	Jacqui Jackson
Catherine Russell	Jayne Lawrence
David Taylor	Jo Hargraves
Debbie Attwood	Karen Smith
Diane Miller	Penny Fletcher
Gabriel Smith	Peter White
Graham Cook	Scarlet Mae
Ian Large	Sylvia Tidy-Harris

There may be others to whom I owe a debt of gratitude, and I apologise if I've missed you out.

Notice of any suggestions, corrections and errors will be gladly received.

Please email aceguidetopacking@gmail.com

Bill Tidy isn't just one of the most gifted cartoonists around, he's also one of the most prolific. He produced so many great cartoons for the Guide that there were simply too many to fit around the text. But it would be a shame if we didn't share them with you, so here are the ones we couldn't squeeze in!

Fishing at Sea

Bird at Security

Musical Coat Hangers

Not Much Room

Personal Trainer

Wellington Rescue Display Team at Glastonbury

Sun Oil

70% Proof

Matador on a Plane

Florence Nightingale